Waking October Leaves

Reanimations by a Small-Town Girl

Books by
VIRGINIA V. JAMES HLAVSA

Poetry

Squinnied for a Sign   (1992)
Festillifes   (1992)
Waking October Leaves: Reanimations
   by a Small-Town Girl   (1993)

Criticism

Faulkner and the Thoroughly Modern Novel   (1991)

Waking October Leaves

Reanimations by a Small-Town Girl

Poems by

Virginia V. James Hlavsa

TIME BEING BOOKS
POETRY IN SIGHT AND SOUND

Time Being Books
10411 Clayton Road
Saint Louis, Missouri 63131

Time Being Books volumes are printed on acid-free paper, and binding materials are chosen for strength and durability.

Time Being Books is an imprint of Time Being Press, Inc.
Saint Louis, Missouri

ISBN 1-56809-000-5
ISBN 1-56809-001-3 (pbk.)

Library of Congress Cataloging-in-Publication Data

Hlavsa, Virginia V. James, 1933-
    Waking October leaves: reanimations by a small-town girl / by
Virginia V. James Hlavsa. — 1st ed.
        p.   cm.
    ISBN 1-56809-000-5
    I. Title.
PS3558.L38W3   1993
811'.54 — dc20   93-5219

Cover design by Kathryn McDaniel Smith
Book design by Ruth Dambach and Lori Loesche
Typesetting by Lori Loesche
Manufactured in the United States of America

First Edition, first printing (October 1993)

Acknowledgments

Grateful acknowledgment is made to the editors and publishers of the following periodicals, in which some of the poems in this book first appeared: *Commonweal* ("Obligations"); *The Dalhousie Review* ("The Corn Mother"); *Descant* ("The Trick of Treating"); *Journal of Poetry Therapy* ("Rages," "A Gathering of Fathers," "Out of It," and "The Creator"); *Lyric* ("Declaration of a Virgin Voyeur"); *Manna* ("Looking Backward"); *Plainsong* ("Animal Crackers"); *Psychopoetica* ("Concert Thoughts," "Shameful Things," and "Smashing Old Doors"); *Tapas* ("My Mother Gave Me Thunder"); *Without Haloes* ("Hamlet's Children"); *Thirteen Poetry Magazine* ("Among Berbers," "Lovers Abandoned," "The Runaway," and "The Tenor of Ten-Year-Old Boredom"); *The New York Times* ("Feminine Endings").

For all their help in getting this manuscript into shape, bouquets of thanks go to my brother, Keen James, and to the staff at Time Being Books, especially Lori Loesche, Sheri Vandermolen and Jerry Call.

To my mother and father,
who, among other things, loved me,
and to John Donadeo,
who, among other things,
knew I could shape that love, those things.

Contents

Part One: LITTLE SISTER

Part Two: BIG MOMMA

Waking October Leaves

Reanimations by a Small-Town Girl

Part One:

LITTLE SISTER

* This symbol is used to indicate that a stanza has been divided because of pagination.

Prologue

The Trick of Treating

The old witch twitches to get in my back door.
Her black shadow on the sill spikes the porch light.
I hear her scratching, searching for cracks.
Her laugh seeps through the door, like oil.
She taps her nails, enchanting, "Let me in, my dear,
    let me in."
I see the knob turn slowly.
I clot, holding my breath, my gaoled heart.
All is still.
I tiptoe close; I put my ear to the door.
Smaller than I, she moans at my breast.
I lean down to the keyhole.
I see an eye.
I spring up, swing back, panting for more doors.
But then I hear her weeping, weeping.
Someone — I know who — is being mean to her.
I know I must let her in.

Lovers Abandoned

I had thought that no daughter could
take my place, who was there first. Wrong.
Separately, first my gem-eyed
mother, then my father, his hands
too large, made daughter number two
number one. I had not reckoned
the reckless love of lovers abandoned.

Containing Losses

The mice and I shared the attic. When I
opened the upstairs door, I would wait for them
to scurry to their places before I ran
to mine. It was a seat in a dormer
where I could read a book or look out over
to Smith's farm, cresting our shared hill, where
my dad and I would horseback ride. Now malled,
the Smith farm is gone, the calm fields to gummed
pavement, the handsome barn to hustler's shells.
The kids use the woods for drugs.
                                        But I lie.
I seldom sat in the window seat. The horse
ran away with this sport. My dad ran away
with his fancy. Besides, like the Smith farm,
I only dreamed I could be so contained.

The Creator

Godlike, I made happy families in my youth.
I made them all the same. Christmas morning,
I would look through the unreflective glass
of the fast trolley, out across the fields,
frozen snow-white, at the pale strings of light
framing the houses and the bright trees within,
splendid with kind mother, attentive father,
loyal brothers, sisters, all giving and
receiving my gifts. Then late Christmas night,
shutting out my own brothers, my mother and me,
I would cup my eyes against the trolley
pane and see the same lights, now shaping pines
inside and out, lining the humming homes
like links of candied stars. Too bad all those
helter-skelter lives like mine never knew
the peaceable kingdom I had fixed them in.

Displacements

I walk down steps. To my left, breath-
taking, a child-sized crate, a surprise,
just for me. But what is in it?

I walk down wide stairs, the heavy
wooden crate, left, in the dining room.
What does it hold? My heart contracts.

Walking down the staircase, at last
I see the room bare, the crate, packed
plates. Displaced, I'd framed myself in
playhouse, all my joy bolted there.

Rages

When you dip into a past, slip
deep in the currents of the day
that loose and wash away old vague
doubts. Take my first felt appendix.
My mother lost it, or did I,
playing too long with my own pleasant
lips? She did try to protect me,
slapping my hands: that was the rage
in those days.

                              Appendix number
two was surgically removed.
According to my dream last night,
when the man approached my bed, knife
in hand, I wedged the walls with my screams.
The operation was performed
because, mother said, I had not
been eating well. That was the rage
in those days.

                              Appendix number
three just disappeared. My father
moved away, then my mother moved
away, while I was taken to live
among strangers. When I returned,
it was gone. That was just starting
to become the rage in those days.

Power Lines

Spider woman, I rise early to tug
this thinnest thread — what I have, all I have —
out of my gut, hitching the crosshatches,
connecting there to here to trap the flies
and butterflies, my bracing food for thought.
This time, drawn from coils: my little girl dresses.
They cover the white cotton panties but ride
above the knees. They do not let me slip
down the banister; they keep me off slides.
I can't shinny up trees or scram over walls.
On bikes, I must tuck a lap between my legs.
Marbles are out, and forget mud. Dresses
are what boys lift, as much for a tease as a peek.
But when I squat down and the nervy wind
flutters before, beneath, or behind my skirt,
I sense the electric voltage below.
From my open wound, lines will be unwound.

Feminine Endings

Boy, this little sister packed a punch. But
then I had a friend in high places. My
father, tall as Lincoln, would call me Cap'n
and pull me high above my two older
brothers, and he'd say, "So you're gonna be the
first woman president?" And I'd scream "Yes!" And
then he'd say (I heard it once at forty),
"Are you Daddy's good little girl?" Well, my
boxing gloves turned soft and pale, and I punched them
so they rose again, up into bread, right?

Outings

Crossing the streets
that crossed so many meaning streets,
    you went up the steep steps,
        through the large, heavy door,
into the high-ceilinged, gloomy room,
    motes afloat,
past the breastworks,
    with the grim dragonladies,
        shushing down at you,
(folks who no doubt knew your folks)
to the dark alcove on the left,
    barely lit by the small,
        green-capped lamps overhead,
where you could sit right down
    on a step-up
and pull out the tall book
    from the S shelf
        one up from the bottom,
opening the window to the light:
    And to Think That I Saw It
    on Mulberry Street.

Declaration of a Virgin Voyeur

Oh, Robert Carver, my prickly bear!
Oh, I do love the prim ribbed back
                    of your tendered hair
                    rising in square crew cut.
Beneath is the desk, etched with grind,
old ink holed, pencil racked. But
                    you're ahead, bristling, blind
                    to my first grade gape.
Oh, do not turn your polar eyes. I'd
have only a faint brush with warm nape
                    fur — less, only eyed —
                    the more, in folds, felt.

The Cover Girl

After my house was taken away,
I was so hungry all the time.
I would take stacks of Ritz crackers
for the Velveeta cheese. When the box
ran out, I'd paint peanut butter
on shredded wheat — when it was gone,
on my fingers. I nibbled at
the fingers themselves. I sucked my thumb.
All of my ten-cent allowance
went to candy, especially the long-
lasting chews. Given two nickels
for the Sunday school collection plate,
I licked one in vanilla cone.
A "found" dime flew into two scoops.
Soon I was a fat little girl.
One of the boys — Danny (It's a name
I will never like) Tomlinson —
loved to call me "lard in the can."
When I faced him, arms akimbo
(Now I know why he piped), he would
look away, his own round face, bored.
Well, it was more than I could stand.
I could cover up my dad's trips
with strange ladies, my mother's pinched-
lipped silence, my two big brothers' too-
removed double-dealings, but how
can you cover up lard in the can?

Stealing Home

I put magic in my childhood the day I saw
the small girl's bike, leaning against the schoolyard fence.
Although almost too small for me, I dubbed it perfect.
With my father having left me, my mother busy
with her own becoming, my time was no longer
on a lead, so I got on the perfect small bike
and rode away. I rode all over my small town.
I rode down to my aunt's, showed it to her, I guess,
overriding her questions. Head straight, I raced past
my father's office, across from the courthouse, and down
Court Street to our old house, where I waved to Mrs. Fretz,
our old next-door neighbor, who used to bake special
small pies, just for me. Then I looped down to lower
State Street, where some kid called "Hey, Jamesie!
    Where'd you get
that bike? Hey, Jamesie, Lucille's lookin' for it," and I,
pumping fast to the fading, "Hey, Jamesie, are you
in for it!" That night, summoned by mother, a double-
barreled policeman filled my living room. The next day,
informed by mother, my teacher stood me up before
the class to crown me for life as the worst first-
grade thief she had ever known. Amazing, they all
missed the real wizardry, my charmed flight back on that
little girl's bike, to restore my little girl's world.

The Mirror

The tall mirror, oval, stood by itself.
You could swivel the walnut frame, tilt it,
and see yourself from the ground up. It gave
you a queenly look, body turned, chin up.
But lying in bed, I could look in it
and view my mother, lying in her high bed,
propped up, brushing her hair (a hundred strokes
a night) or snapping her Zippo shut (from the man
I thought was her "bow") for the day's first drag.
Once she caught me: "I see you watching there!"

But who was that fair, dark-haired young woman?
What did she know of me, who wears her name?
What — how could she bear to have me so close,
reflecting on her, except as a mirror?

Shameful Things

Two things drove my mother cray zee.
The worst was when I sucked my thumb.
It felt part of me, like my tongue.
The next was when I pulled a crisp,
white sheet between my toes or fingers
or beneath my fingernails. It
felt so cool. I tried to sneak, but
mother usually caught me and down
would go her foot: "Stop it, ViVi!"
What puzzled me was why I was
so bad. Or so mad — no one else
I knew did such things. My mother
didn't think on what puzzled her.

Out of It

My big brother Wynne got impetigo.
His skin was crawling with sick
little bumps and pus and then thick
yellow crusts which, he was lucky,
he got to peel off. Mother had to rub
purple stuff all over him.
They got it all over the tub.
When they went into the bathroom,
I tried to follow. "Mind your own beeswax,
Little Miss." I leaned down
to the keyhole. "Peekers might get poked
in the eye!" I never got to watch
the good stuff. I never even got it.

Parens

Spelled, the summer evenings
enclosed us like parentheses
of pearl shells, bright with soft
air and not having to do. And
if the father was gone,
even the mother could try her smile,
even the big brothers
could give a kid a turn at bat.

My Mother Gave Me Thunder

My mother gave me thunder
and lightning. As she sat
on the porch, the dog, Patsy,
beneath her chair, she would be
smoking and talking calmly
or carping. No wonder
now I turn off the light
and pull up the chair. The screen
expands. The show is mine.
And by counting the miles between
flashes and crashes, I'm
at the controls, captain mid night.

My mother's thunder gave me
(now that I can count the miles
by that time that reconciles
sound and sense) the will (or
what she called my willfulness) for
managing her storms. She
once tied me to a chair.
Issue forgot, the sight
of my wrapt fury made her
eyes shift. I knew the fight
was done. The rock learns its power
by flooring the fire-damned air.

Learning New Words

Since my mother's last visit, I had learned
five new words I knew I couldn't say and then
I did: shitpooppeebowelstits. As one
who had literally washed the figuratively
dirty words out of my mouth and memory,
she seemed strangely underwhelmed by my litter.
(Did I even sense a quickly cornered smile?)
I expect she blamed the new bad company
I kept, the family she had left me with
in the house that smelled poor, although I liked
the large hot air register to dress on that warmed
your leggings. But there I was, rucked up with
Bully Mary, Marble-eyed Frank, Polio-
leg-braced Buddy and, rarely, Margaret,
pretty and slim, my former sitter gone scarce,
who once, walking me the three miles from town,
took a ride from a man she knew, who then
drove off the highway into a quarry and tried
for a kiss while she pleaded *The child!*" while I
sat in the truck, my cheeks dark with the words
I needed to know to flush out my dirty thoughts.

Lunchtime Lessons

My head well above the oak desk, my back
to the rows of need, I hear the hissing
behind me: "Hey, Fatso!" "Whacha want, Creep?"
"Marn, is that your *mother's* dress?" "Yawanna
cookie, Doreen?" "Why doncha flap those ears,
Dumbo? I'll betcha could fly." I had come
to the altar with my grateful offering
for her reigning presence, her long face framed
with pinned blonde swirls. My present, tidbit news
of myself. But now I watch, beneath the torqued
face, the two long pink-glossed nails, solemnly
fetch the small fleck of food my mouth had flung
onto the pure printed page between us.
The lesson plan had just become Disgust.

The Birth of Aesthetics

My eyes slide along the yellow-glazed curves
of stone lips, cold cheek and a head cracked in two
like a chick-abandoned shell. What a work
of art! Titled "Fragmentary Head of Queen,"
it is even eyeless, for my voyeur's
eyes. I cannot abandon the looking;
the looking wantons me. Those full, thick lips,
like pillow on pillow or breast on nippled breast,
they lure my mind's fingertips to both what
it is and what it is not: the balmy,
warm skin and the hard-ridged relief. But what
is it I want? When I raise the scrim, I
see my beautiful young mother at my
classroom door. In this miracle (I have not
seen her for weeks), she lifts me out of the pack.
She comes like the Blue Fairy, Pinocchio's
guardian angel, who appears just when
all is lost. At the sight of her dazzle eyes,
my heart takes in her seemliness: the high,
sweet curve of the forehead, the beatific smile.
(She used to say that friends called the painting
of her and her son "Madonna and Child.")
Well, I cannot abandon the wonder of it.
I cannot abandon the ecstasy —
without falling afoul of my ugly rage.

The Tenor of Ten-Year-Old Boredom

As I waited for news of myself,
the books could quiet and stir me,
luring me with their lives within.
But coming to, looking up, out,
impatient for casts of my own, I
would rock the gray porch rocker across
the gray porch boards: ta-ta-ta-ta-
TA, ta-ta-ta-ta-TA, feet a-
gainst the silent railing, the railing.
Across the clearing, the sun-struck
woods wheedle with sounds profound.
Surrounded by sinewy, hidden fires,
I am ready to torch my heart.

Smashing Old Doors

Once my brother noticed me. By that time
I was wild, someone holding me while I
thrashed arms and fists. The holding let me be
wilder still until we surged, holders and I
near the front door, and I slam-banged my fist
through the thick pane. Amazed, we stood
around my bloody hand, magnificent red rage.
We staggered on shards. And now at my side,
my big brother found his first kind words.

Lost Brother

Before unbound, we faced eath other, wound,
cowled in child- nighthood of play mate.
Now, from without, the slow white knobs of hate
slide, lump, collide and slide again,
    dumb and sinister,
under some dreamed-up water weight.

But then, within, there was foul play —
was kick and pinch and scratch and sock
and back-pinned arm and hair-yank shock
and brittle thumb on bone-dry gum.
    Total war. Single combat.
Keen-eyed Batman, I had you in holy deadlock,

until you, one warm noon, pushing ahead,
step on my neck, awake.
Underwater, I, bursting, upbreak,
feel your buoyed surge, your silvered flick;
    thickly I, rising too,
breathing at last, gasp after your lost wake.

The Runaway

I wanted to run away
the day I heard their murmurs,
low, holding the living room.
Sitting on the curved high-back,
Mother and the man, whose army
coat lay stiff on my bed, were
sandwiched, with what meat between.

So I ran away to the movies.
Claudette Colbert danced and
Christians were fed to the lions.
I ate jujyfruits in the dark.
On the bright bus, the blank cheer:
at least I would get home late.

Animal Crackers

Mother would laugh when I shrieked,
well, I really barked, when
her new husband would creep
up behind me and jab
his fingers in my waist.
She would laugh when I cried,
well, really howled, when he
would grab my face and rub
his whiskered chin across
my cheek. They would both laugh.
Often I would laugh too,
switching my animal calls.

The Violence of Small-Town Inmates

Most school days at noon, marked by the courthouse
clock, I would walk across the courthouse lawn
(towered building and lawn long since crushed)
from my high school (now just a parking lot)
to my father's office at 84 North Main.
(Must get that address down, now that he's gone.)
I came for a letter from Herbie or Paul
or Steve, at least so I thought, waiting. Crossing
the lawn, I would seek reports from large brown leaves.
Often, I would pass inmates of the county jail,
guarded, raking. I could almost catch them,
stuffing bags, flicking their eyes at me and mine.
To my right my turreted grandmother whiled.
To my left, at the five corners, the civil
war monument, a warning, was circled, unmarked:
on one side, the gaping firehouse, where men
peered out, volunteers, foreseeing fires;
on another, the Rexall Drugs, where I ate lunch,
a grilled cheese on white and a vanilla shake,
even this violence tamed by the weight of waits
for letters that seldom came, amid unmarked
monuments, while old leavings, all stuffed within,
ready to burn, set me crossing the lawn,
starved sick for a word, noticing the flicked eyes
of jailed lives, crunching dry leaves underfoot.

Everything in Store

It was a sign, "Everything In Store $10."
When I had everything in store, I was still unsure
what was in stock, what on display; what I would be
selling, what giving away, while my two big brothers
had adventures. They had hitchhiked across country,
which I couldn't do, so I picked up hitchhikers,
telling them tales of my two big brothers, waiting for hours
for a lift, making myself "somebody's sister, boys, you know,"
no easy lay. So no one bothered me. They just looked,
until one day a couple of boys, their merry eyes
flying, said, "Uh-huh" and danced right past my rationales.
The more I talked, the more the talk drifted. I guess
they were wondering who would be first. As for me,
my smiling face was leaking chagrin; I was about
to be found out. How could I keep from shaming us all?
The place they had chosen to disembark was near town.
It was getting dark. As soon as I pulled over, the guy
in front was halfway down my pants, when all at once
he said, "Hey! You're wearing the rag! Why didn't you
tell me you was wearing the rag?" That he could use
that word! — Like he had everything in store for *ten*
bucks. But what really raped was that *was*. And my sense
that beneath his kid's crudeness lay a kind concern.

Unseeing

With a winter eye, across the scabbed pond
through the brush, I see two black trunks of trees,
angled like legs, a knobbed knee, and those shanks
are striding with animus, branched tail held high,
leathered limbs, like Puss-in-Boots, deep in snow.
Once long ago, my gamine self was moved
into a room, planned by a fancied Mommy
and Daddy of a good little baby girl,
with pink wallpaper with little white woolly
lambs, all in a line, leaping over fences,
counting down to sleep. I saw each cluster
as part of large, heart-shaped faces, with eyes
(no nose, no mouth) like X's, watching me
as if blanked, stunned, by the little black sheep
they saw, hating hearts, hating lambs, hating
smoochy, smoochy hugs and spanks I saw from
the little man (who laughed at what he knew
of girls), who came to live down my mother's
lane. When I lit out, my little sister
was moved to lie beneath the woolly lambs,
leaping fences, counting down. Did she, like me,
need to unsee all the whelped shapes facing her?

Epilogue

The Raree

You know the shot. It's V-J Day. The girl,
all in white, has been hanked, whirled
away back in a real Hollywood clutch
by that taut young sailor. Not much
to say about him, farmer's hand,
but the outfit makes him a leading man.

Her dress is slack-waisted and crisp, hem broad;
her legs, white-stockinged, thick-seamed, heavy-shod.
Hair's in an upsweep. For all that, she's classy. The clean
hands, Hinds Honey and Almond creamed,
push at the brassy, dark-uniformed flirt
and pull at her own light-uniformed skirt
that covers up all that tomfoolery beneath.

Eyes shut, lip slipping on lip-covered teeth,
coarse, briny warm — well, for all the passion
it wakes, it could be his elbow. But fashion
the two of them hamming, side showing,
both part of the Victory, both knowing
their part, including, apart at post-camera snap,
to look forty ways, wipe mouth, straighten cap,
while the fellow for fellows says, "Whoo-ee. My, my!"
and the nurse claps the back of her head, laughing, shy.

Part Two:

BIG MOMMA

Prologue

The Reckoning

You might be surprised to hear
what I must do on Halloween night.

First, I take the stars between my teeth.
When I bite down, the sparks simply
tickle my gums, crackle my ears.
But I can smell-taste the sulphur.

Then, when the moon lurks on the pond,
I lurch to the edge.
Before I can dive in the mad-white hole,
the water shivers, aware,
slicing up my great escape.

So I butter my body with frost.
Belly up, wrapped in the skein of a vole,
I wait on the lawn for a cloak:
perhaps the bowels of the fox
or the throat of the great horned owl.

It had better come soon before my mom returns,
back from the dead, helmeted,
reckoning to read my poems.

Timed Thoughts

Stuffing my mouth with popcorn stacks:

I am not thinking about striding down a familiar street,
    my father's large, slender hand, holding mine,
    when time stood up, bowed, and asked, "What next?"

I am not thinking about brushing my mother's long,
    electric hair, smoothing her high, exquisite forehead,
    when time muscled my arm, staving off Siberian sheets.

I am not thinking about bundling among fireglowed friends,
    lying next to the funniest boy, laughing, when time
    turned twice to curl up, purring, in my pupal loins.

I am not thinking about the large bed, with the baby
    sleeping warm on my belly, on my bowels, when time
    sweetened my tongue with honey, my breasts with cream.

I am not thinking about a Sunday afternoon at four,
    with the door on the lock and the phone off the hook,
    when time squeezed out bounty shouts like a concertina.

I am thinking about propping my feet up for a good read.
I am thinking about stroking a cat in my lap, maybe two.
    I am thinking about a time without time.

My Old Virginia Dare

The girl drives by in the small-tired go-cart,
allowing herself a half-smile. I was all smiles,
driving the tractor, all business,
those two weeks on the working farm.
The cow was something else. With my own breasts
relaxing, relating, I felt a faint squeamishness,
so I grabbed her labby tits,
and I squeezed and prized,
while the master hand laughed.
Nothing came, her smooth warm hide a wall.
(All mothers must be leather-bound.)
But those machines, hacking and bucking and
— Whoa! — running away,
so I could stall out, so I could start 'er up again.
To this day, the logy smell of new-mown hay
still lifts me high on that buzzing tractor seat,
shaking the very Virginia out of my pants.

Waking October Leaves

For Louis Daniel Brodsky

Amid red and gold canyons of October leaves,
aglow in the late afternoon light,
I am charmed by all this old age, childed
again, taken back to the dead times,
to the young old people who canyoned my world.
Beached beneath their familiar faces, I often
did not know their names or even if
we were related. They lived on familiar-
sounding streets: Church, State, Union,
which I could not find, or in nearby *villes*:
Kintners —, Carvers —, Garden —, which I could not place.
They spoke a strange language, but they would poke
their Esperanto into my getaway car, my talking,
sweating face: howareyoudearwhereareyourhandsome
brothersnowwhoareyoulivingwithwhatisyournewmother's
nameisshenicewhereisshefromwhenweretheymarriedandhow
isthatnewbabyofherswhatishisnamehowoldishenow
whendoyougettoseeyourownmotherdearIknowshemustbe
verybusybesuretogivehermyloveIthinkofhersooften.
Thank you, I will. Thank you. Thank you. Thank you.
I often wished the cat had got my tongue.
But all those bright leaves have dropped or hang,
dry brown, on cold limbs, their own show and tell,
told. And now I flare with the mixed tones
of their names, their places, their tongues.

Obligations

There is a house I must often pass, so
ugly — yellow with black spots and stone lions
and retread planters — I have trained my eye
to look across the road or up or down
or anywhere but there or it will fix
itself on my mind like the lunchroom sight
of other kids' uneaten crusts would make
me gag with poor-child obligation. Bad
enough when winter-bare, it's worse in spring
or fall, for then, in front, a sweet young tree,
filigreed, wild, raises its slender arms, reddens
its tender leaves, pointing out, pointing in.

The Real Estate

Can ice be real, bound by a rune rain barrel? —
glazed, a marbled cloud, cast from swelling drops,
from slow, warm spills by chill, possessing night
which wrings the very oil of finger bone?
Innocent days! We said, Who would poison
a rain barrel! Yet Shive's boy uncurled and died,
lay mirroring sky.

                    After this while, I poke
the plank of ice, chunking the edge like a tomb,
triangles plotting circled deeps. Then
even this solidness melts. Absorbing form,
the mirror disclouds, and knowing, confessing, the bond
lies not in innocence, I chant: Rain barrel,
rain barrel, poisoned cup, frozen fare, loosening up;
Lord, in the draught I must drink, ring me round.

In My Place

When I am orphaned by the night,
tired yet awake, alone, I get up
and let the dog out and in and let
the cat in and out. (They must
wonder what's where they are not.)

Sweeping the stars aside, my night descends.
Brought low, cast out by the deadened blank
of my neighbors' blinds, my mind tries
doors within, feeling the thick dark
for signs of life, this time a bright

shack, dirty, with broken seats and ashtrays
filled with folded butts. And comic books.
Since it is late, I wait for a cab, reading,
alone with a man, unnoticed, until he says,
"Aren't you Wynne James's daughter?"

Pleased, I say I am. I am not shy.
"I know your dad from way back. He's tall!"
"Yes," full of the joke, "we call him flagpole,
but he says that's only from the side!"
"Well," he says, pulling his chair closer,

"you're a big girl." I smile.
"How tall are you?" I tell him.
"Well, you're a big girl. Such strong legs."
He puts his hand on my leg. He
crouches. "Such nice, strong legs."

His hand moves under my skirt, up my thigh
to the beat, "Such nice, strong legs,"
repeated, his eyes close. "Don't," I say,
my voice faint. "Such a nice, strong girl."
His finger scratches my crotch.

With a noise outside, the face is gone.
Untreated, the red burn turns black.
He and I put me in my place, all right.
When I am orphaned by the night,
I hardly wonder what's where I am not.

A Gathering of Fathers

On Father's Day, I dreamt I saw the man
of the north, my Uncle Norman, now long dead.
"Oh, come in," I said, taking his handsome face
between my hands. "Mother will be so glad
to see you." But it was me he'd come for,
smiling, ready to set right his anger
from years ago when, exhausted, he'd left
me and my favor asked, unanswered, the smile
turned cold. Then I sat next to the man of old
(the Miller who taught me Chaucer) in concert,
carefully penning my own note to tell him
what a good teacher he had been. But he
said, pointing to a long, blank space, "What's this?"
"Ever the English teacher," I teased, but
he ignored me. He had found another mistake.
Then I knew my husband knew I was at him
again — a symptom. Time for more treatment
from the man of the hour. But I left all that, rushing
across a deep rage — no, range of snow,
crisscrossed with wire meshing. I crossed fences,
laboring, rushed, ticked at myself for not
taking the path around, angry at my mad
career, at the double cross of all those fathers'
leavings, leaving me cross on Father's Day.

The Darling Girl

Although he left me with his leavings,
   I was my father's darling girl.
His date for a weekend at Buck Hill Falls,
   I could step up on his large, stiff
shoes, and we'd dance to the applause.
   Leading lady to his leading man,
raised by his laughing arms, I could
   squash his hat on my head, then his,
cockeye his glasses, kiss his smooth
   cheek (the whiskers barely at bay),
then wrinkle my nose at the camera.
   Wearing his boots and rain jacket,
I could sing, "You are my sunshine,"
   shuffle under his umbrella
and his clapping, "Encore! Encore!"
   So even now, when my plied forehead
hits me like the crack of the crisp
   leaf I am, every mirror lies,
and when I lie next to the heart
   of my love, forty shapes glisten,
silky with caressing and wise
   with recalling all I have forgot,
   all I have wanted to overlook.

Copper Spoils

I think her name was Billie. At least I want
to call her Billie for the Billie Jean
King she might have been. She was tough. Coppery
hair, fair skin and a long, thin face with pouched
cheeks, she captained many teams. I can see
her the year she died, about twelve, fingers
spread on the basketball like some airy
cantaloupe, orange outside and in, the skin
smooth and hard, the bounce light. I see her pause,
hunched, choosing, all control in the fine arms,
the thin wrists, the watch with the black leather strap
(Did they bury it with her?) keeping time.
I see her flick the ball away with a slick
twist of her palms. Serious, she took no
notice of me, a watcher, nor I, especially,
of her, no more than the others in the class.
I can hardly recall the others, now
more than forty years past. They are all like
copper pennies grown dull from nonuse. Only
Billie comes to life, made bright by the rub
of my glancing mind over her polio death.

The Word in the Sword

Because my father tipped his hat,
I still curtsy my head, a small-town
maneuver, deployed instead of the sword
and more manageable than the word,
the word that lies hidden within
the sword's shape, shaping all our
neighborly wars, like all wars, by
rumors of wars, the more quiet the worse:
water only whispers on the boil.

Elizabeth's Gifts

Now come to a calm, safe season, I think back
on Elizabeth, my father's Anne Boleyn,
who, trying to hug my cold shoulders, would call
herself the "wicked stepmother," hanging
her hat on my nail. In fact, I hated
her kindness, her Spockian care, a rebuke
to my mother, off careering on her own.
A queen-maker, she would have me bake cakes
for "the boys," my two older brothers, who,
twitting "your lowness," would treat it like hardtack,
a comeuppance I cheerfully bruited about.
In *her* dishes lurked mushroom and leeks, like slugs.
Modern versed, she would "use" psychology. Once,
heeding my tears, she said the divorce was not
my fault, unwittingly stiffing my starring role.
A drinker, Elizabeth slept deep, so when
her infant son cried at night, I would scream
"E-*liz*-a-beth!" trumpeting my rich rage.
But she bought me Mary Janes (*not* Buster Browns),
she taught me to test fudge (I can feel the soft ball),
and she saw to it that I took ballet,
closing off a big double room for me
to practice my tour jetés. There, camouflaged
as a nine-year-old heavyweight, I danced —
to Beethoven's Fifth — my own choreographed
tale, swan-shot with romance and flight, I
danseur, danseuse, each boosting the other's beauty.

When my mother could finally take me,
she could take me. When, as a teen, I could
no longer take her, I asked to return,
Elizabeth's buddy, on the buddy
system as her own marriage floated loose.
Although a plank in my father's platform,
I also piqued her interest for myself,
eager now to hear of Freud and Mansfield
and Kierkegaard. And the man she would call
"your dad." A Middle West liberal, she
would tell me tales, maybe tall, of his success
*

in business. "The people" loved him, maybe awed
by his desire to help "the little guy,"
his democratic decency. (Probably,
ever the wag, he also loved to screw
his fellow oligarchs.) But we would laugh
at his French beret, the small-town shocker,
or at his tall self, mounted on horseback,
his long legs dangling, his earflaps down, moving
at a stately pace, as if a deadpan
backdrop for a play by Kaufman and Hart.
Then we would go make scrambled egg sandwiches
and sit before the fire, our faces alight
in the dark, our bare feet curled beneath us,
weaving with the hearth's miniature fireworks,
the soft shuttles of mice. Or she would throw parties,
then treat me to the gossip or tease me —
to my squeamish delight — that this or that man
had been flirting with me. She was drinking more.
Sometimes I sat while she wept, wringing my hand,
her blue eyes red and rolling, her fair face foxed.
Flattered, I also felt stiff. This buddy
could never be bad enough. When I smoked,
it was Kools, which she styled "medicinal,"
unlike her own iniquitous Camels.
No doubt, she suffered, a thinker, a writer,
famous for her real estate ads in the *Times*.
Always late, her permed hair wild, she would tug
the upturned collar of her tan trench coat,
and hip her slight frame forward like a boy,
flipping her funny retorts, her tongue in cheek.
Wicked indeed. Smart, she could make you smart.
But it was the awkwardness that made you bleed.

When my father moved on to his Jane Seymour,
I finally left. Her children were growing
more interesting, more needy. But I took her
with me, years later learning by my son
how to be both the one hand and the other,
the prince charming and wicked stepmother.

Strange Lessons from a Liberated Woman

My Great Aunt Dodie lifted weights.
Aged 91, she would sit up on
the table in the dining room,
her short legs dangling, with four or five
pound rolls around her ankles. Each
lift caused her pain, although you would
never know it from her face, which
stared back at a world full of challenges
to meet which she had mostly met.

When she could, my Great Aunt Dodie
sold us life insurance, a life-
long crusade she had taken up
back before social security,
back when a widow could well be left
destitute. "With children to feed
and no family, she might have to
take to the streets," was what she said.
We did not dare ask what she meant.

Well in her forties, my Great Aunt
Dodie married the German she
had hired for her ascent of Mount
Blackburn. They had been caught in a storm.
He once complained that good Prussian
names had been taken over by Jews.
She admired long-dead Harding. When
they divorced, the family asked why.
"It's none of your business," she said.

Hearing I had car-camped along
the Alcan Highway, my Great Aunt
Dodie willed me a collapsible
silver cup. In the Twenties, she
had, for a month, ridden on horseback
deep in the woods of Alaska.
"What did you do for mosquito
bites?" I asked. "I simply didn't
scratch them." Now I know she was right.

On Becoming a Woman

When my Nanan, prying answers
about her son's latest, would take
my arm while we slowly gimped along,
it felt most peculiar, as if
I was to be the man, even a man
she clutched with some entitlement.

When my stepmother would cozy up
to have a woman's gab or, drunk,
squeeze my hand and cry or even,
sober, hug my shoulders, planning
recipes, I would glance away,
wondering what my next move should be.

Or when teams of bloomered girls tore past
or the slight nymphs, who could prize up
out of the pool, basked in prides or
even when they turned their grid eyes
at me, all I knew to speak of
was race relations, um, world peace.

But when my father sat at the head
of the table, chewing slowly, when he
would look at me and flick one brow,
one smile, while he lifted one cheek
and farted, this was when I felt
most like the woman I would become.

A Stranger Becoming

My hands are bony, the fingers long,
the skin smooth. Graying, now I am
become my Nanan. Tall woman,
dominant boned, she had the large Barbiere
nose and parts of her wound round the house.
De Camptown Races darkened the parlor.
It was her long hair they cut from
the gears of the grandfather clock.
Her phone was encrusted with grime.
Nevermind. When she started hitch-
hiking, my dad had to put her away.
Too bad. But even when she crashed
at the last, worst time, she pitched you
with those sharp, black eyes as she sat,
nodding, lips pursed, whistling a faint
do dah, crab-fleshed legs spread. But see
here, her skin, and the long hand bones.
Racing towards her, I drag on her breath.

The Gnostic

I know now the sound of crashing,
of crushing metal on metal,
dividing time, like creation,
into darkness and light, into
blank and sight. An expectant Eve,
an afterthought, swelling with slants,
I had heard the thick groans of planes
ripping the sky while I doted
on familiar freckles or probed
my unfamiliar face, always
avoiding eyes. Then came the cast,
broken by crash. When not-knowing
becomes knowing, we sniff our own
burning flesh, now a blinding flash,
and hope others will sift our dust
for bones. Disgardened, care-taking,
we hear the distant ones nearby
all dying to know, all dying.

Nice Guys Are Soon Forgotten

This storm, this sudden blinding shower
of stones, after my father had died
(after his long, furious failing
as he worked and left his will),
this storm sent us under a bridge.
Ahead lay the mountains of Maggiore.

This lake is blue, they say.
My father's eyes were flame blue.
Now black, the water reflected on clouds.
But when they were trundled off
and the sun marched down to the lake,
I saw the glass-glazed blue,

warming. Photograph that, I said,
photographs fixing the willful dead.

The Longings

The sun aprons the far cliffs, bustling before
the plunge into long night when we lie alone.
But we have known this dark all along. In love,
we should fly like mallard pairs, intent on nesting,
yet we lie unwoven or we promenade,
coffee cups in hand, pretending public
preoccupations. As a child, I whined,
"Take me with you. Please, let me live with you,"
playing with my mother's clean, cool fingers.
One visit, I couldn't stop singing or humming
(until she snapped at her monomaniac),
"I don't want to set the world on fi-yer.
I just want to start [*beat*] a flame in your heart."
As for my father, royalty entered the room
with his step, his glance, his warm hand. But like a king,
he was rich with other promises to keep.
("You went away and my heart went with you.
I say your name in my ev vree prayer.")
Oh, the longing, the longing. A savored voice
on the phone can hollow the heart. Pleas sent skyward
lose their weight in space. Yet though I would hug
myself to squeeze out the empty places,
though I would throw my leg over blackouts,
still, I can shrug off the hand groping for me.

The Corn Mother

I

If time could be cooled and sliced, quivering
from its jelly mold, with all our leftovers hung
randomly within, truth would be found lying heavy
at the base, fleshed out, naked, head turned,
weeping — Oh Dear! — for its own ugliness. What is it
the young man missed? What else need we know?
Beauty may be truth, but truth may be ugly,
lying cold and naked, lying wasted on the floor.

II

This year I know I will have the honored role
as the last sheaf. At last I will be the Corn
Mother, the crone, feared and reported by all.
I felt it coming. When I was running loose
over the field, a surly wind, I knew buffeting enough
to strangle the stranger's children,
those crimp-haired, black-eyed babes I had long ago
pulled from my loins, unsheathed and abandoned,
unable to name them in my gnarled disgust.

III

Now I will be left for the strong young man,
the clumsy reaper, he who has been tricked.
They will call, "He has got the Bitch!"
"He has got the Old Woman and must keep her!"
"Dolly! Dolly! Dolly!" Even though it shames him,
even though his mollusk cheeks burn a dark red,
even though, like all carters of carrion,
he will not let his eye meet your eye,
he knows he must chase me down.
The burly boy knows he must embrace me.

IV

Once a sneaking child, finding a forbidden room,
came on a large young woman, a girl, seated,
staring at her with blank, black eyes.
A brood shame, kept close by a small town, developing
pearls, the girl grew daily in the child's mind.
As her own body ripened, the girl too spread
in womanly thigh. Both eggs cycled with the moon;
the stalked blood in both convulsed and cooled
like the white glint in the girl's dark eye.
For all the old child knows, she might be there still,
pulsing to the sun-planed, rock-cold moon.

V

My breasts hang heavy with all this bidden,
forbidden fruit. As the rest fall and the winds push,
wafting my top-heavy desire, I swing full
as the first glow of coming for coming again.
My seeds will sack me. The color of dun,
they string the smell of the sun across
my scrawny throat. Laughing, droll, they will call,
"Thrash the Old Maid! Stroke the Neck!" When he is done,
they will dunk the burly boy, muddy his face,
roll him in dung, for his own sake, and for his girl.

VI

She — He — My woman's erection is a body arching
for arrow. Together our desires dare
for the bull's eye, secret, staring, daily death.
But the woman not loved is not worth the loving.
When my lover loves me not, when he shrinks from me,
I must shrink from myself. In my ballooning meat,
I am become a beached whale, drying, my white
carnivorous teeth hinged for the fit of firm flesh.

➥

VII

So what in the end does the fat lady sing?
Listen to the hiss of the Corn Mother:
the old truth is a child unmoved by a mother
unmoved, is a woman unloved by a man unloved,
is a man shamed by a woman shamed, is an old
witch, strange to herself, seeking the bliss
of the chosen, seeking clips to the young,
with time's friction firing her rank sprawl.

VIII

Seizing me, the burly boy's strong arms *umarm* me.
He calls me "dear" as he slices my rough crutch.
Cut on the diagonal, interlocked,
my thick beads will form a faceted diadem
for the prettiest girl to cast aside, to burn.
She will remember them when she learns that beauty
may be truth, but truth, even reaped by myth,
yet sinks heavy as dust on the threshing floor.

On Deadlines

At five below,
rushing down
to meet a deadline
where the mother-of-pearl
fused sky
is hinged at the Bronx,
I think back on Madie's
last warm days.
The tumbling clicks
of the maple seed propellers
pleased her so.
Her head tilted,
her smile cleared,
rude intelligence gone.

Jangling Jays

The jays are out jangling today,
going on over passersby.
It's fall. It's warm, but the hunters
are coming. My mother's gone now,
and Tom and Scott and Isabelle.
All in one year. How the bodies
pile up! You'd think we were at war.
Well, we are, shooting our lives at
each other, sounding off in our
not-so-dumb way. At times the wounds
could stop you dead. Mind you, I know
the enemies engaging me
are on my side.
                    But I was marking
the jay. His squawk, about as raucous
as mine, says, Damn you, passersby,
and again, Damn you for passing by.

Rescuing Mother

My mother went "in sure and certain hope
        of the resurrection."
Beyond, she planned "first, to see my father,
        whom I adored."
Then she would meet my stepfather: "Not once
        did we have words."
But I've got my mother spread all over
        my living room floor.
Stretching on my Persian rug, I hear, "Red
        is my favorite color."
It's ruby ("my birthstone"), like the rustling
        gown she passed on
for me to play dressups. And yellows are
        nowhere in sight:
"Yellows among reds set my teeth on edge."
        I've got "a place
for everything and everything in its
        place," just in case.

Late Communion

Ever after my father'd left,
my mother lived in half-houses.
But as she loved to say, moving day,
the first thing she'd do was to plant
her mint. She used it with ritual
pleasure, stirring it with a long
silver spoon into her iced tea
or making jelly for lamb. It was
a taste I never acquired. Still, years
later, striding down through fields near
a creek, I stopped, transfixed. Heedless
of snakes, I foraged through the tall
grass, looking for some lost breath. Finding
the green weed, I brushed one rough leaf
on my cheek, on my lips, crushed it
on my finger tips and breathed deep,
regretting my love turned on the scent,
wanting to take in the flesh itself,
to drink it, to eat it, myself
consumed instead by my passionate
communion with my mother's desires.

Aging Certainties

My mother said I snapped all the buds off
the peony bush. I said I didn't.
She was so certain. So was I. We were
both as certain as those tight little heads.
But now, fifty years gone by, all I have
to go on is my old certainty. I do
recall the bush on the side of the house,
but that's all. By rights, I might rest my case
on my half-century of certainty.
But mother's dead now, and anyhow,
nothing seems quite so certain anymore.

SAD Calculations of Ever After

Q.   A.

1. In the old days, in movies,   (underscore
   some mommies left their kids,   correct
   who needed them. Even   answer)
   though those mommies were bad,   A: two
   how many years did the kids   B: ten
   wait for them?   C: forever

Q.   A.

2.   In the old days,   (circle
   in movies, some mommies stayed   correct
   with their kids, who needed them.   answer)
   Even though those mommies   A: two
   were good, how many years   B: ten
   did the kids stay with them?   C: depends

Hamlet's Children

Let's say Hamlet survived all that carnage
    and had then his own tale to tell.
What better tablet for griefs and regrets
    than the minds of his own children.
And could they not but agree: O most foul,
    unnatural affronts: murder,
incest, treachery, the *ten* thousand shocks
    that that one man, now another
face-lined Paul Scofield, had been heir to,
    and we so blessed in kind father,
devoted mother. And so we would plead,
    obsessively, Tell us again
how your mother betrayed you, and then your
    petal-mouthed Ophelia (and you, her).
And tell how your father's wraith first appeared
    (led stair on stair, our hearts wrung white)
and laid on you the burden of revenge
    when you were but a chit, not much
older than we — how ill-equipped you felt,
    when, clamped to damning foreknowledge,
your mind orbed between being and nonbeing,
    between fathers lost, mother's lust.

How weary, stale, flat, unprofitable
    would be our own complaints, our taints!
Rather, ever pacing the ramparts, we
    would pronounce our own Never again!,
conjure up our own play within the play,
    or assure the furied old man
that all roads are wrong in this Hamlet world.

When I Caress Another

When I caress another
                with my eyes,
I am of my father's eyes.
I see them, caressing me,
and being caressed; I feel them,
                the gesture
like the sweet curve of an egg.

When I caress another
                with my eyes,
I, the author, become the bearing
matrix of my author.
Transparent it is transpiring is
                the gentleness
of my father's eye-caress.

Looking Backward

My father's eyes, wide
within his glasses, light blue
wounds, knowing I lied.

My father's eyes, small
without his glasses, the skin
tender, the folds, thin.

My father's eyes, half
softened with love, half turning,
the face, half open.

Rewinding Sound Bites

Mother

With her crystal eyes, her voices,
and her hands, bright familiars,
she is like that lavender tin —
the Louis Sherry candy box —
full of odd buttons,
washed of wild, sweet choices.

———

Father

Before the fire,
his deep voice, soft as smoke, warm
as hushing white ash.

Among Berbers

Here I stand, among Berbers, who wear
the shade of their hoods. Overhead, thick
trunks of sycamores, shorn to the nub,
are stuck with shocks of gray-green sticks.
Around the square, dark eyes, eroded
like rock fists from the dark land, stare
at me. I might tell them that beneath
my strange costume, like them, I carry
my father's height, my mother's laugh.

Concert Thoughts

"Another woman to curse the world," proclaimed Auntie
at my birth, and then, spinning a brass bowl on its edge
for my pleasure, she'd add, "someday, another damned
woman driver." Bossy, she was, like all the women
in the family, or so said (say) all the men, and proud
of her strong, anti-suffragette opinions. But I
hardly heard her. Rather, I must have thought, "I know
what I am. I am a wounded man." Years before, before
I could even remember, when I'd still been flat
chested, and, well, *featureless,* so I wasn't my mom
and I wasn't my dad, I'm sure I saw my little black
homunculus drop off into the potty. It had to be.
Even the smell was mine. And I seemed to recall,
especially in dreams, the *feel* of having that pen.

Here, before me, in concert, Angel Angelorum,
madonna with spread knees, holding the infant son, the dead
man — No — just the swooning cello, from here it looks
as if, elbows out, having been given back the child's
little man, you can play on yourself, knees as wide
as grief or joy, dragging the drugged sounds onto your lap
from taut, well-tuned, quick-fingered files within,

                                        encoringly.
But then, we women can come many times. We are large;
we can accommodate the multitudes of men
who tunnel through us passageways to other men,
loving the lamp that darkens the direst holy well,
while we women, absurd thought but true, recalling
our own mother-fit, play manly for mainly ourselves.

Hooked by My Own Line

My women lie beneath
the surface now — Mother,
Madie, Aunt Dot. They are
in another world, quite
beyond recall, response.
Yet their power bends the
tall sedges at the shore's
edge —
    Rubbish! That's the carp.

The Upstart

Tall, I almost always hang
over the mattress. Bold,
my letters overleap all bounds.
Trying to corner me, my First
Grade teacher had to shout *OUT*!
Tying me to a chair, my mom
lost it, and me besides.
Solid walls can't hold me.
I plunge through plaster,
through stone. My ceiling's
twice gone through the roof.
Off in my books, in my words,
I live largely — yea, hugely —
beyond the real world. But
then, grounded, I'm rude: I
interrupt friends or I'll
grab them, eye-fasten them,
prying up all their brass tacks.
And now, with my time/space
contracting, contracting,
I would ladder these lines up,
over the walls of my life.

The Real Goods

Watch the water where you've heard the splash.
You may see the fish, rolling up again,
as if to slip on, try, his future life
although he looks like a thick cardboard prop,
and he makes the pond tuck, tuck at the edge.

Running from me, the poet said, "You're good,"
the wispy word raising my hopes the more
to be cast down as my own poet within
felt the old superwoman/ego shaft.
To be good, I must give up being good,
my old comfort traversing shepherdless wastes.
In such valleys of death, if I would sing
my own psalm and have the pebbly words worn
smooth by many tender mouths, I must leap
from this sluggish film again and again,
seeking, Goodness!, the surprise, fully arched,
suspended in the last, light, killing air.

Lines for Assembly

On reading Eamon Grennan's
"The Coming Day"

Still leaves stir, nervous in the pond's
reflection. They suddenly read like lines,
but lines scrolling too fast to read
or to write. The poet says his day's
world opens before him like a blank
page. I guess. My day dawns in the stacks.
Whole tomes tilt my way, spilling words,
lines, prints, scenes, cross references, asking
to be reassembled, this time
with proper covers and spine braces.
Take this frame: Mother is shuffling
away from me, her hospital gown
open, her back pale, her bottom
sagging. That's to be rebound, chaptered
with her leap, lift (*bang-bang*), bright-
edged dive (*chunk*), her resurfacing smile.

My Mother's Loving Cup

Not long after she had died, my sister
Mary sent me my mother's silver loving cup.
Arms akimbo, it reads "AGNES IRWIN SCHOOL
SWIMMING MEET / 1922 / WON BY
Virginia Marsh Freeman." Its shoulders, high
like mutton sleeves, have come off their anxious
symmetry, the right one now slightly shrugged
from being smacked around ? not wrapped too tight ?
My mother's own loving cup would rarely
runneth over, although, with the lifting
of her motherly lid, she did grow ever
more cheerful, more giving, more forgiving.
My mother's loving cup. I want to be
ironic, but it was not her only
case of achievement, and besides, out of all
the times with her, or (mostly) without her,
I do recall the warm days she took us
swimming — to the pool — she — like the water
itself — sparkling — or, riding in Mary
(years later, my half sister would get her name)
Maneely's rumble seat, out to under
the bridge at Lumberville, where, there ♪ beside
the Delaware ♪ we swam and picnicked, and
my brothers would cup their hands and squirt me,
and I could scream, dancing with the cold and
the heat of my richly physical complaints,
and my mother could take my side, seeing
herself in me, as I now see myself
in her and pass the loving cup, reinscribed
To: **Virginia Marsh Freeman** (when she was)
James / From: **Virginia Victoria** (when I was)
James / *She Often Swam on My Team* / *Often*
        She Wanted Me to Win the Loving Cup.

Epilogue

Reversions

In this Bleak House behind my eyes, my father's
divorce of me plays and replays through the courts,
ever appealing with each new love's leaving.
Still angry? In the beginning, my fury
at my begetters was so murderous, I had
sentenced it to life, chucking the key. At the cell's
center, abscessing: How could such good people
do such awful things.

                An unformed life, crashed,
acts like an ambulance, forever damned
to reversal rush, as if the outrage
to the naked child is so deforming,
she must seek change not by caring, curing
new skin, but by some daring sleight, uncrashing,
such as, say, unmasking father's mother,
to show him that the witch's own ambition
could only be lashed to his sail. Indeed,
with what we now know from all we have
suffered, expanding forgiveness into
beholding, we might unmask the whole midnight
procession of strange ancestral parodies
of parents until we could begin again
with dawning light for the affable "Be fruitful;
                          multiply."

Born in Doylestown, Pennsylvania, in 1933, Virginia V. James Hlavsa received her Ph.D. in English and American Literature from the New York State University at Stony Brook and taught for many years at Queens College. She has written extensively on Faulkner: her book *Faulkner and the Thoroughly Modern Novel* was issued in 1991 by the University Press of Virginia, and she was recently Guest Editor of *Women's Studies* for a special issue on Faulkner and Women. In addition to writing poetry, which has appeared in journals such as *Descant*, *Commonweal*, and *The Dalhousie Review*, she tutors writing to learning-disabled young adults. Married for over 40 years, she and her husband Richard have one son, David, a graduate of Princeton and the University of Washington.

Also available from **Time Being Books**

LOUIS DANIEL BRODSKY

You Can't Go Back, Exactly
The Thorough Earth
Four and Twenty Blackbirds Soaring
Mississippi Vistas: Volume One of *A Mississippi Trilogy*
Forever, for Now: Poems for a Later Love
Mistress Mississippi: Volume Three of *A Mississippi Trilogy*
A Gleam in the Eye: Poems for a First Baby
Gestapo Crows: Holocaust Poems
The Capital Café: Poems of Redneck, U.S.A.

LOUIS DANIEL BRODSKY and WILLIAM HEYEN

Falling from Heaven: Holocaust Poems of a Jew and a Gentile

HARRY JAMES CARGAS, Ed.

Telling the Tale: A Tribute to Elie Wiesel on the Occasion of
His 65th Birthday — Essays, Reflections, and Poems

ROBERT HAMBLIN

From the Ground Up: Poems of One Southerner's Passage
to Adulthood

WILLIAM HEYEN

Erika: Poems of the Holocaust
Pterodactyl Rose: Poems of Ecology
Ribbons: The Gulf War — A Poem

TED HIRSCHFIELD

German Requiem: Poems of the War and the Atonement of a
Third Reich Child

RODGER KAMENETZ

The Missing Jew: New and Selected Poems

NORBERT KRAPF

Somewhere in Southern Indiana: Poems of Midwestern Origins

JOSEPH MEREDITH

Hunter's Moon: Poems from Boyhood to Manhood

FOR OUR CATALOG OR TO ORDER
(800) 331-6605 Monday through Friday, 8 a.m. to 4 p.m. Central time
FAX: (314) 432-7939